HOW TO READ

HOW TO READ

POEMS BY
THOMAS RICHARDSON

Thomas Richardson (signature)

Friendly City Books
columbus mississippi

For information regarding permission, please email info@friendlycitybooks.com.

ISBN: 978-0-578-87140-0
Library of Congress Control Number: 2021906959

First paperback edition May 2021

Cover art by Alice Pieschel
Cover and interior design by McAnally Creative
Written, designed, and published in Columbus, Mississippi
Printed in the United States of America

Published by
Friendly City Books
118 5th Street North
Columbus, MS 39701
www.friendlycitybooks.com

Contents

Acknowledgments

None of us learns to read wholly on our own. Perhaps it starts with the songs our mothers sing to us when we're babies. Maybe it's the tall tales of our fathers and grandfathers around the campfire. For some, it's the whooping and hollering from the pulpit or the cadence of communal prayers that soaks into us as we start to make connections in church bulletins and wispy bible pages. As we grow, so do the voices influencing us, helping us find words of our own so that no one gets to speak for us. These helpers are our teachers, our classmates, our friends, the strangers on the bus; anywhere and everywhere language goes, we're learning. It would be impossible, then, for me to thank everyone who has been a part of my reading and writing journey, but the following list comprises those names without whom this collection of poems about reading would not exist.

First, I must thank my parents, who spent my early years reciting lines of classic, contemporary, and obscure texts for God knows what reasons when all I wanted to do was play second base for the Atlanta Braves. They surrounded me with books and showed me by their example the value of spending an entire career helping people find their own voices. I also need to thank my sister, Cameron, who made me think having a big vocabulary was cool, and who kept her patience when I thought every quiet moment was an opportunity to practice humor.

Hillary, my partner and my most trusted reader, has kept this collection (and me) alive with her patience and persistence in love. I owe her so much more than I can possibly give. My son Emmett also has my deep gratitude for reading with me and teaching me so many new ways to think about the world.

My MFA classmates and professors from Mississippi University for Women encouraged me through countless drafts and bouts of self-doubt, and their fingerprints are all over this collection.

I thank them for challenging me and loving me. A special thanks goes out to my thesis readers: Kendall Dunkelberg, T.K. Lee, and Jacqueline Trimble.

I am grateful for the support of all my colleagues at New Hope High School and The Mississippi School for Mathematics and Science, friends in Columbus, and members of the Mississippi Philological Association who have read and critiqued my work. Hope DeVenney, Mary Wiygul, Alex Pieschel, Brian Hamblen, and Jonathan Evans have especially nudged this collection forward.

Finally, I must thank Emily Liner and the crew at Friendly City Books, who took a chance on this collection and are making great strides to promote reading in Columbus, Mississippi. I am in awe of what they are accomplishing.

Versions of some poems in this collection have previously appeared in the following publications:

Cantos: "American Education," "The Bees," "Elegy for Matthew and Jonathan," "The ER Staff Listens to My Heart and Me," "How to Read in Gastonia, North Carolina," "Seismology," and "To My Wife, My Love, Who Brought Home Lite Mayo"

Deep South Magazine: "Self-Portrait as Sacrifice on the Diamond"

Intégrité: "And All God's People Said 'Amen,'" "A Child Wrestles with Theodicy in Mississippi Springs," "A New Verse," "Someday I'll Love Thomas Richardson," "This, Too, Shall Pass," and "When They Finally Let God Back in Schools"

POMPA: "Discovery," "Eupora High School Gym, 2002," "Grad School Rag: Novel Discussion," "Grading School," "Inside and Out," "A Mississippian Mingles at the Academic Conference Happy Hour," "Oxygen Mask," "Reading Shakespeare with Teenagers," "Red Letter Bible," and "When You Find Me Writing in the Coffee Shop"

The erasure poem "Public Hanging" derives from the Associated Press article "Mississippi senator's 'public hanging' remark draws rebuke" (first published Nov. 12, 2018).

PART 1:
HOW TO READ IN GASTONIA, NORTH CAROLINA

SEISMOLOGY

I want to build a poem
from an earthquake.
I would start with the
tremors under toes and
the spastic ripples in a teacup.
Then maybe my speaker would
shout to his wife that
this is the big one
as they ran for cover
under their antique dinette.
I'd have to fill the middle section
with the requisite sounds—
some rumbles and rattles,
crashes and screams—
as the bookshelves unfastened
themselves from their studs.
As they waited out the furious
convulsions, my couple would
conjure the conceit—some
philosophy on fixedness or
the fault lines of the heart.
Peace would come and they
could sweep up the rubble
and patch their fragmented selves.
But I've never been in an earthquake.
I don't know the subconscious routines,
the preventive feng shui
born from a house set jelly-legged
by the whims of rocks.
I have been able to trust my steps
and walk in straight lines,
barefoot on calm soil.
For that I sit blank-paged,
praying to the floor until it
opens up and swallows me whole.

HOW TO READ IN GASTONIA, NORTH CAROLINA
for Ed Cushman

In the minivan, Dad mutes Handel's *Messiah* so Mom
    can read to Sis and me.
Good professors teach literacy when killing time
    between stops on I-85,
cultivate high-browed appreciation for *les mots justes*
    on printed page.

But outside the Amoco food mart—a temple of
    Sun Drop and Copenhagen—
a hand-scrawled sign over wire-topped barrel warns,
    "Red bats from Taiwan!"
and stands sinister obstacle for sojourning families in
    need of restroom relief.

Mom goes first, creeps up to the sideshow cage, and
    peers over at sign's promise.
Sis and I wait just behind, paralyzed by demon-eyed
    beasts our minds draw up.
We position ourselves to sprint back to the van if
    rusted wire doesn't hold.

The attendant cackles behind the glass at our
    hesitation, lets out a wide-mouthed
yodel that seems to whistle past his tooth,
    Right here is a real pack of idiots.
He hoots as we find the sign's truth: red foam
    baseball bats, made in Taiwan.

We smile, wave to acknowledge the wit hidden under
    that Earnhardt hat.
We shuttle back to the interstate and sit quietly—
    no book for a while—
because thanks to a sage in Gastonia, we now know
    how to read.

SOUTHSIDE PANTOUM

Columbus, Mississippi

When I moved to town,
I wore rubber boots and nothing else.
It's a good thing, too, a witness said.
You have to be a freak to live here.

I wore rubber boots and nothing else
because naked don't mean nothing
    when you're four.
You have to be a freak to live here,
stripped down to raw gothic.

When you're four, naked's just a word,
but it's a portrait of soul self:
stripped down, raw gothic,
like my neighbor in the Rebel uniform.

It's a portrait of soul self,
and a good thing, too,
like my neighbor in the Rebel uniform,
when you move to this town.

THE BEES

Two good boys,
the kind parents show off in polite company:
Yes, ma'am, all A's.
I'll see you Sunday, sir.

Good boys could roam
Mom and Dad's college campus after school,
raid vending machines, explore science labs.
They could wield Wiffle bats
in search of green space.

But that day the ballgame yielded to
buzzing from dusky chapel stairs.
Curiosity found a swarm:
clouds of black and gold blimps,
floating,
plump and unfazed by our presence—
bumblebees don't sting.

We exchanged cautious glances,
but what's a boy to do but swing?
After all, they just hovered there,
our eyes trained to
pounce on hanging curves.

I sent the first one
spiraling in a puff of pollen.
My friend followed,
pelting bee after bee off the
back brick wall.
We traded cuts and sides of the plate—
switch hitters like Chipper—
until the minute's frenzy left us with
no more targets.

THOMAS RICHARDSON

We surveyed our destruction:
hundreds sacrificed at chapel door.

We told. His mom, my dad.
We may have cried.
We wanted to go to The Hague.
Instead, we were sentenced to
growing up.

I read this morning that
bee populations are dwindling.

Continuing its rise, though?
The population of
good boys.

THE SUB

If you come in here a fool—
wild eyes, flashin' all that lip—
you'll go out of here a fool.

You'll find out I'm old school,
ain't put away my whip,
if you come in here a fool.

Boy, you think you're *fresh*, you're *cool*.
Got no home trainin', can't get a grip:
You'll go out of here a fool.

Young lady? Look so fine—a jewel.
We'll see you at The Landing Strip
if you come in here a fool.

I'm the old gray mare, but I ain't no mule.
If you think I'll let crazy slip,
you'll go out of here a fool.

Go on, then, try my every rule.
Act a clown, a bum, a trip.
If you come in here a fool,
you'll go out of here a fool.

THOMAS RICHARDSON

WRITING LINES

```
I will not talk back to the teacher.
I will not talk back to the teacher.
I will not talk back to the teacher.
I will not talk back to the teacher.
I will not talk back to the teacher.
I will not talk back to the teacher.
I will not talk back to the teacher.
I will not talk back to the teacher.
I will      talk back to the teacher.
I will      talk      to the teacher.
I          talk      to the tea    .
I          talk      to         her.
I wi  n        back    the teacher.
I will not      ba      the         .
I   ill          back to      tea   .
I will            ac  t              .
I will                          ache .
I will          back          cher.
I will not                  he   a    r.
I will not                          .
I will not                          .
I will                              .
```

EUPORA HIGH SCHOOL GYM, 2002

Off the bus, we find the usual heavy air of
    stale popcorn,
the faint notes of mildew from Jordans
    left in gym bags,
each doorknob, threshold, bench
    streaked with rust.

In our locker room, teammates—lank-legged
    Black and white boys—
tape ankles, slip on jerseys that should
    label us the enemy.
But the bigger battle, a cold
    culture war,
heats the stands naively marked
    "Visitor" and "Home."

On one side, Black fans back their all
    Black team,
punctuate dunks, and echo
    every *swish*.
Across the floor, white parents ignore
    court action,
flip through magazines, braid
    hair until
their all white dance squad takes
    the halftime stage.

At intermission's end, waves of camo
    and blond hair
pour through exits as our dribbles and
    sneaker squeaks

reverberate through a
    half-drained gym.
We visitors can't explain the tableau
    we're performing
between the baselines, but it feels
    like Mississippi.

When the buzzer sounds, teams shake hands
    and we bus back home.
Eupora tidies up, shuts off the lights, and readies
    for another game tomorrow.

A CHILD WRESTLES WITH THEODICY IN MISSISSIPPI SPRINGS

When tornadoes came, Sis and I moved
with lightning speed to grab transistors,
wedge on batting helmets, and anchor ourselves
under pillows and blankets in the claw-foot tub.
Our mother read Psalm 91 by flashlight
as the overheads strobed, popped, and failed.
You will not fear the terror of the night,
or the arrow that flies by day.
We could always hear the train—not a
dissonant horn, but the violent rumble-chug
of twisted air laying its own tracks—closer
or in some other family's yard.
A thousand may fall at your side,
ten thousand at your right hand,
but it will not come near you.
When the silence won, every time,
we unfixed our knees and elbows from
cold porcelain and set out to
check on neighbors, report downed lines.
We'd find chimney bricks in drainage gutters,
pine needles pierced through trunks,
but everyone we knew whole and thanking God.
Next to my Cheerios, the sprawled morning
paper ran death tolls,
photos of oaks dissecting Camrys,
someone's grandmother
missing near the county line.
The Lord has his way in the whirlwind and the storm,
and the clouds are the dust of his feet.

THOMAS RICHARDSON

DISCOVERY

In ninth grade Tech Discovery,
a new month meant a new module,
a new partner. I moved counterclockwise
among the cubicles arranged in concentric circles
and reached "Ecology."
And Becca:
she, blue eyes and braces, and I, five feet flat,
face slick as a peeled onion.
We scanned the manual for
objectives that lined up with the equipment;
small town Mississippi tax bases can't
always keep the litmus strips stocked or
the microscopes in focus.
But we found the VHS with the Sharpied
label "Water Cycle" and popped it in.
We should have known from the opening credits,
slap bass, smoky sax, names like
Nikki Jade, Randy Steele,
we would find no explanation of transpiration, evaporation.
At first, we laughed,
pushed back the nervous heat in our cheeks,
swiveled our heads to see if anyone—
maybe Mr. Poynter—caught our peeping.
But the camera zoomed in and magnified
every goosebump, brought closer
each rhythmic collision between smooth, sinewy legs.
Neither of us lifted a finger toward Stop or Eject.
Instead, we sat in silent awe of the physics,
their bodies a perpetual motion machine,
another thwap bringing new ripples across the skin's surface.
And the sweat—*Dear God*, the sweat—bubbled,

spread, and pooled as breaths (ours or theirs?)
heaved in tectonic push and pull.
It wasn't until the bell rang that we noticed
we were holding hands.

THE HAIKUIST LIVE-TWEETS A SCHOOL LUNCH BREAK

Jock peers around Stacks,
finds nerd tutoring girlfriend:
a dance for Darwin.
#rumbleinreference

|

Coach scratches and sniffs,
scribbles plays on stained napkin,
scores fattest paycheck.
#lessenplans

|

Ink-stained teacher sits,
sinks teeth into ham sandwich.
Brrrrring! Heaven on hold.
#thebelltollsforthee

TO ASHLEY MILLER: SENIOR, HEARTBREAKER

Dear Ashley, Crusher of Dreams:
I know that when you called me cute
you thought it was a compliment.
When you looked up from the salad bar
(the Salisbury steak too crude for us)
and smiled at me, you could have said
almost anything, and I would have
melted into bliss, like that marshmallow
Mrs. Davidson roasted over
the Bunsen burner fourth period.

Yet you chose *cute*.

Babies are cute. Petits fours are cute.
Kittens playing, old couples kissing,
our homecoming king trying to
pronounce endoplasmic reticulum—
all cute. But I'm a man, Ashley,
I'm fifteen. I can list all the
presidents in chronological order
and all fifty states alphabetically.
I can shred on the violin and recite
Sonnet 18 by [my now-shattered] heart.
Not to mention I just bought a razor.

I've seen you with Bruce Wiggins, his
arm around you while you wear his
leather jacket. I guess he does have a
way of making his long hair fall in
just the right places, but are you not
worried that his slack-jaw drool will
drown you? You should have seen that
Neanderthal's fire finally starting to flicker

when he looked at the diagram in health class:
Girls have three holes? Still, he must be
good at sex. He told his troop of apes
he takes chicks to *the third dimension*.
Enjoy the honeymoon in *London, France*—
I know he'll make a good husband and father.

And when I deliver your fifth child,
Bruce's spitting-image, I hope
you'll look into my cute face and
curse the day you decided to call
me that word, instead of writing our
own romance over a carton of milk.

MEMENTO MORI

for Martha Brown (1924-2020)

In last night's quarantine daze,
I shuffled books from coffee table
to side table, back to coffee table.
I boxed my son's toys by color and shape,
restacked board games in our hallway closet.
It was the rattle of the Scrabble tiles
that pulled me back to all those nights at
Swoope Drive, when you taught young
grandchildren the value of the two-letter word—
QI for thirty-three points, ZA for forty—
that less is often so much more.
But your best lesson came before the game ever
started, when you asked me to retrieve
the board from your closet shelf.
I pulled a stepstool from behind coats—
old gabardine and tweed—slid to the side
baby toys four generations' hands had
held, and found the game under a new
dark-stained walnut box. *For my ashes*,
you told me, as you caught me fiddling
with the lid and measuring the box's
depth with a sweep of my fingertips.
You need to know where it is when I'm gone.
I stiffened at first, then laughed off
the unease bubbling in my belly
and promised I wouldn't forget.
Back at the card table, we arranged
letters in concentrated quiet, only
breaking the peace to offer complaints
about the hands we were dealt—
too many vowels or too few—
but my mind kept drifting to the box
your brother care-crafted with the same
hands he must have used to pull your

hair and toss your doll over the fence, or
carry your school books and cradle your children.
What could I have known of prudence?
I had so much time; the years flowed
ahead of me in colorful rivulets.
The box, that small, dark, and
empty thing, opened its mouth to all the
futures I had yet to write in childhood whimsy.
I spun a coated letter between my knuckles
and waited for my turn, for someone to
clear this table and sweep all these words away.

HEAT HE HOLLOW GEE HUFF RAISING
(ETIOLOGY OF PHRASING)
for Emmett

Mice sun
    can odd yeah treed,
        buddy nose thief Al you've
            theme ewes sickle frays,
                hay whelp laced whirr din
                    prop her hoard her.

Heap Oz sis
    tool his hen
        Winnie ear stones sand
            writ thumbs,
                Dan says win heel hikes
                    beet sent I'm.

Though sue half Ben Abe hill
    two reed ford heck aids
        fork hit lank wedge him her Jess sass
            hound beef whores height,
                mew sick bee four wry ting.

         THOMAS RICHARDSON

PART II:
HOW TO READ SHAKESPEARE WITH TEENAGERS

AMERICAN EDUCATION

To teach is to imagine
a classroom scattered with bodies—
mouths twisted, chests full of holes—
and go on rambling about poetry.

A classroom scattered with bodies
too young to enter a warzone
goes on rambling about poetry
and fights death with flowers.

Though too young, they enter a warzone,
wrestling with meter and metaphor,
fighting our deaths with flowers,
and planting beauty in neat rows.

Children wrestle with meter and metaphor,
smiles twisting, their chests full of holes
for planting beauty in neat rows.
To teach is to be able to imagine.

READING SHAKESPEARE WITH TEENAGERS

I.

Romeo, Romeo, let down your hair,
Juliet said back in Bible Times
(somewhere between Vietnam and World War III).
Why didn't he just write in plain English?
He sounds like a douche:
More like, Shall I compare thee to a Summer's Eve?
Wasn't Shakespeare gay?
Mercutio is gay.
To be or not to be gay?
Lady Macbeth wears the pants.
Do not tell me Ophelia jumped
In the water for that freak.
Ham-and-Cheese Omelet needs Zoloft
or at least a date with Freud.

II.

On top of undersized desks, The Bard arrives.
He swoops in through ears,
carves past thickets of estrogen and testosterone,
and plants himself on the banks of
head and heart's roiling rivers.
Love, Beauty, and Yearning pitch their tents
beside Ambition, Desperation, Deceit.
We—student, teacher, artist, instinct—
commune at this tempest-edge,
and for a moment the centuries converge.
We stay until the tedium—maybe trigonometry—
calls us back to our routines,
but we'll return.
Shakespeare lives here now.

6-4-3

Cross step to
back hand to
slide stop to
four-seam to
spike twist to
arm whip to
lead man to
foot drag to
jump throw to
full stretch to
big mitt to
turn two.

HOMECOMING

At the pep rally, our gaze falls
where unlikely architects hoist and stack:
Bronzed legs meld, form pride of Giza.
Eyes of all ages—classmates, teachers, dads—
lock in on the capstone, the senior,
whose skirt remains freshman-sized.

"V-I-C-T-O-R-Y, that's our Spartan battle cry!"

Dancers draw stares with uniform
gyrations, indicting every onlooker
who can't help but follow each
bounce and drop. God help us
if one makes eye contact.

"V-I-C-T-O-R-Y, that's our Spartan battle cry!"

Passion swells as cymbals crash and
hiss to bass's boom and snare's rattle.
Tubas sway for brass chorus:
crescendoing trumpets and trombones.
Flutes stand no chance in this fervor.

"V-I-C-T-O-R- Y, that's our Spartan battle cry!"

Hysteria reaches its climax:
Chiseled warriors parade through
pom-poms—do we bow as they
pass? Flashbulbs illuminate
parental delight, and screams
pierce and echo until the last
waterboy emerges.

"V-I-C-T-O-R-Y, that's our Spartan battle cry!"

We know for some this will be
as good as it gets.

THOMAS RICHARDSON

GRADING SCHOOL

Connor failed his essay.
You wrangle
the paperwork
(a five-page proof
that you did your job),
and you decide that maybe
Connor did not fail his essay,
after all.

But then Connor will think he's a good writer.
And just look at his fucking face,
his pompous cheeks contorting
each grin into a taunt:
I didn't even read the book, he'd sneer.

So mark the paper up,
make it look like a Tarantino film.
Leave no doubt you're in charge.

Connor will be turned off of your class.
Cue the mounds of carbon-copied referrals:
When prompted to begin working,
Connor boasted, "Writing is for pussies."

You'll call his mom and
haul your notes to the office—
Document everything, the vets told you
in teacher school.
But with Principal Good Ol' Boy as mediator,
your three degrees stand no chance
against Mom's v-neck and yoga pants.

So you click the red pen,
offer tepid praise,
scribble a few notes about usage
to show you tried,
and give Connor a B.

AHMED MOHAMED, 14

A 14-year-old boy says he was just trying to show off his engineering skill when he brought a digital clock he had made to his new high school in Irving, Texas. But Ahmed Mohamed was detained and reportedly suspended from school, after a teacher thought that his clock looked like a bomb. –NPR

They took him to a room where four other officers were waiting. When he entered, one officer leaned back in his chair and said, "That's who I thought it was." –The Washington Post

"We live in an age where you can't take things like that to school," [Chief Larry Boyd] said. –The Atlantic

Police spokesman James McLellan: "He kept maintaining it was a clock, but there was no broader explanation." –The Dallas Morning News

Ahmed wanted to build:
stripped wires, charged circuits,
toted his hobby clock where it'd be
safe, admired.
Ahmed wanted to impress.
You have to try harder
when you look like him,
bear that name.
You speak up, enunciate,
wear that NASA shirt,
because what the authorities
spewed in schoolroom interrogation
you've come to expect.
In our country, that simple machine,
everyday descendant of the sundial,
needs more explanation than
another brown boy in handcuffs.

WHEN THEY FINALLY LET GOD BACK IN SCHOOLS

He took a seat behind Stephanie and Brad
and Melody, who pulled their shirts
over their noses and cut their eyes,
snickered and whispered with all the other
Stephanies and Brads and Melodys.

When he crossed the room for a
pencil from the bin, Ms. Parsons
chided his neglect and whispered
(too loud) to *take a shower, please*, and
tie those laces if he wanted to *ever get ahead*.

In the hallway, his bowed and shuffling
gait caught nudges from the crowd,
scattering his things across the gray tiles
where muddy sneakers trampled his
anatomy notes and geometry proofs.

After lunch, students gathered at the
flagpole to link arms and sing praises to
God from whom their blessings flowed.
There was no room in the circle for him,
but he listened as they prayed:

*We thank you, Father God, for making us
just the way we are. We ask that you send
us your spirit to dwell among us so
we may do your will on Earth, Amen.*

GRAD SCHOOL RAG: NOVEL DISCUSSION

We're ready to
challenge the hegemony,
plumb intertextuality;
suspicious hermeneutics
set to trouble our reality.

Our class is subversive,
a little bit discursive,
but we're solid on our theory,
you can write that down in cursive.

We talk Foucault, Fanon,
Marx, Barthes, and Derrida,
and if you have no use for Freud,
we suggest you call your ma.

We move from meta to praxis,
turn the canon on its axis,
problematize, categorize,
behind our black-rimmed glasses.

We've got our buzzwords at the ready,
our voices are so heady.
Let's start class already!
Did anyone read the book?

THE HAIKUIST LIVE-TWEETS THE EGG BOWL, 2015

Cooler caravan
moves toward tailgate encampment.
Cowbells beat cadence.
#maroonarmy #distanceparking
|

Morning's meal dangles
from frat boy's face as bros haul
his body dormward.
#earlyexit #brotherlylove
|

Jeb! courts rural votes
with selfies, ribs, and Bud Light.
Tens of fans gather.
#pollinginsixth #pityclaps
|

Lines at Junction Johns
cause grown men to eye trees, shrubs.
Desperation grows.
#intake #output
|

Pregame flyover
stirs spirits already roused by
hot toddy and suds.
#USA #USA #USA
|

The House that Dak Built
rumbles with pyro blasts, bells.
Clanga, clanga, y'all.
#kickoff #earplugs
|

Bibulous Rebel
infiltrates loyal home crowd,
draws stares, sows unrest.
#rebelrousing

|

Tanked Dawg undergrad
sprints past refs, cops, and flips bird
to Rebel faithful.
#fanonfield #notastreaker

|

Potatoes, rice, grains,
nuts, poultry feed, quarterbacks:
some things often sacked.
#noprotection #Dakonback

|

At halftime, rain falls,
plays echo to Bulldog hopes.
Ponchos are sold out.
#21to3

|

"Don't Stop Believin'"
blasts through stadium speakers,
taunts faithful dreamers.
#31to13

|

Only the truest
remain as time expires on
Golden Egg promise.
#nextyeardawgs

|

Evening bacchanal
breeds regret, toxic belches.
Sunday service looms.
#lightsout

A MISSISSIPPIAN MINGLES AT THE ACADEMIC CONFERENCE HAPPY HOUR

after Harrison Scott Key

I'm only three crostinis in when
they ask me to conjugate.
Then the applause—*See, Janet?*—
when I say y'all.
And what even is a mud pie? and
Was The Help *right about fried chicken and Crisco?*
I give a nervous tug on my lanyard
as a crowd gathers, cheese plates in hand.
Someone, emboldened by the quiche,
praises me for *making it* after what must have been
a long dirt road of a life, guiding my wagon
through stifling summers, past all the
Klan rallies and obese pregnant teens.
Tell us about Mississippi; we have to know.
Well, it all goes back to Faulkner, I say,
as I start scouting for loose drink tickets.

PART III:
HOW TO READ A RED-LETTER BIBLE

SELF-PORTRAIT AS SACRIFICE ON THE DIAMOND

Batter baptized in pine tar strides toward plate
while shoe-polished eyes find brother stranded.
This batter knows how his brief appearance must end,
yet he hoists ash bat above shoulder and
scratches cleated toe through red Georgia clay—
        dig and tap, scrape and spit.

He squares, a giveaway, and corners rush in
to seize the ten-foot offering our batter has
deadened down the line, his stirruped legs churning
toward a destination he is not allowed to reach.
He smiles at ump's rejection; brother is safe.

Metrics scorn the bunt, tell us it's a fool's errand—
a waste of quick-twitch skill to lay one down for
only a chance at later reward. But the numbers
cannot feel the dirt-diamond hope that moves
in all of us, begs us to trust that the one who
comes behind will be the one to move us forward.

Praise God for the bunt, and for every sacrifice
and squeeze that pushes us toward home.

AND ALL GOD'S PEOPLE SAID "AMEN"
for Etta Richardson (1925-2010)

When my grandmother died,
the preacher eulogized her coconut cake.
Somewhere between "Psalm 23" and "Blessed Assurance,"
he gave those packed in the pews at
Manly Presbyterian Church
a revival in confectioner's sugar and full-fat milk.
While the Hammond warbled behind him,
the Reverend Doctor picked up speed,
wiped his brow as he reminded every mourner
that the only grace there was
was the grace they could taste,
the kind that paints a sheen on the lips,
and in Etta's kitchen, there was a slice for every
widow, orphan, outcast, and addict.
Into your hands we commend your sweet servant, Lord.
What is love but four sticks of butter, hand whipped
and spread smooth behind an unlatched screen door?

THIS, TOO, SHALL PASS

Bleak-branch Winter
surrenders icy
hold,
bends toward sibling Spring's
embrace.
Though they cannot
stay,
neither mourns
because now
the others come and
take their places,
perform appointed
work.

So let us, too,
in our dreary days,
look for fresh-bud
swelling.
Yet in our
bloom-time
we must admit that
falling
greets us
soon.

A NEW VERSE

for James C.P. Brown (1927-2015)

You even hummed when you ate your grits.
Every wheelbarrow trip, hauling pine straw
or grandchildren, had a soundtrack,
a folk tune from the farm or a hymn
practiced years behind the pulpit.
No wedding reception or graduation
was too formal for impromptu baritone blessings.
But your leaving was too unlike your living:
sterile silence, drip tubes and still hands,
a decrescendo on hospice.

So sing on, James.

Now that you've got your voice back,
hit that Old Man River; let your bass
set the whole earth on a rumble.
When you meet that Sweet Little Jesus Boy,
give him your best Noah's Ark—
he'll join in on the *cock-a-doodle-doo*—
or maybe Froggy Went A-Courtin',
and let him strum the chords;
teach him what we got to learn on your lap.
Ask Precious Lord to take your hand,
and join in the kingdom opry eternal.

IN JANUARY 2021, AN AMERICAN DIES OF COVID-19 EVERY 33 SECONDS

The time it takes to
take out the trash
walk to the mailbox
feed the dog
reheat coffee in the microwave
down a Twinkie
swish Listerine
ignore a YouTube ad
review iCalendar
do enough jumping jacks
shampoo hair
order DoorDash
find keys
buckle child into car seat
walk back to car after leaving mask
send the right emoji to therapist
wash hands and hum "Happy Birthday" (twice)
mix a stiff drink
play a hand of Blackjack
segue to the next Netflix show
piss after night of drinking
read this poem
tweet from the Oval Office
cast a ballot
wish upon a star
hold breath
disappear

ELEGY FOR MATTHEW AND JONATHAN

When sorrows come, they come not single spies
But in battalions.
    Claudius, Hamlet *Act 4, Scene 5*

The slings and arrows of our
outrageous fortune
struck, Fate's sordid regiment.
This conquest of heart—accomplished at one—
pilfered two.
Seeking orders, we call for an AWOL general,
but we are left to bury the dead: futures, dreams
piled in caissons.
Bugle notes limp skyward, yet this is no time for song,
Heaven's ears sewn shut.

So we trudge on, tear-blind, toward sanctuary,
heavy breath and lead strides betraying our pace.
We can't know how long we'll have to march
as bombardment lingers.
But we endure—shoulder to shoulder—
survivors carrying memory.

THOMAS RICHARDSON

RED-LETTER BIBLE

Fly or fry, Aunt Sis chanted at me
all those years before she found herself
on judgment's doorstep.
I never saw it so clearly.

Packing up her worldlies, I browse her
leather-bound Bible—creased, faded—
to find Jesus's lines in red letters.

A moving symbol, perhaps?
Holy words, colored by blood shed for all?

I trace garnet gospel,
reaching for revelation,
to know—know!—
as plain as it's printed before me.

But Red-Letter Bibles are
American inventions, carry my
red-blooded American values:
simple, efficient—
reduce Divine to hue,
prune story to rosy talking points.

Instead, Truth hides in the white spaces
between red letters, where I hunt for meaning
and wait for fiery red tongues to rest on me.

SERMON NOTES FROM THE MARGIN OF MY CHURCH BULLETIN

pastor
past or
post Ra
op star
Pa sort
taps or
raps to
spa rot
to spar
to rasp
or spat
so part
as port
sat pro
sot par
ars pot
op rast
trapos
atorps
aptros
saptor
orpats
po rats

THE HAIKUIST LIVE-TWEETS A SUNDAY SERVICE

Piped prelude fanfare
masks Ruth's mumbled barbs about
Jane's altar flowers.
#blessherheart
|

Acolytes don robes,
march graceful path to candles
deacons left wickless.
#lightunderabushel
|

Pearl left her glasses,
struggles to sing the first hymn:
"Be Thou My Vision."
#nodandhum
|

Pastor reads Matthew,
the Beatitudes, again;
hopes this time it holds.
#blessedarethestubborn
|

Frank sleeps through sermon,
catches prayerful rest until
his ringtone echoes.
#jesus #mainline
|

Toddler snorts and coughs,
drags hand under leaking nose,
dips bread into cup.
#ewwcharist
|

Ushers pass down plates,
blink at pitiful returns,
send them back around.
#muchgiven #muchrequired
    |
Congregants stand for
pastor's graceful farewell charge:
their favorite part.
#brunchreservations #mimosas

'PUBLIC HANGING'

a white
Mississippi   saying: "If he
invited me to a public hanging, I'd be on the front row."

a black
Sunday   remark
for

a bitter history of

the United States,
Mississippi

the most

challenged

no place

lacks

judgment   of our

state

a statue of

white people clapping politely for

cattle

retired

until   resolved

the   years of   longtime

defeats

trying to become

"a very reliable, trusted source"

THOMAS RICHARDSON

Mississippi,

a state known for

people

who

will vote for

Confederate monuments.

INSIDE AND OUT

It starts like this:
You break the buckle,
slip leather through loop,
and I drift,

hurtle really,
like
what was his name?
that orbiter—
Cassini—
that six ton
sweet soul,
who plunged through
Saturn's rings and
debris fields
and mystery,
for us,
snapped photos
for us
to lead us star people
back to our origins.
How do you thank
a machine that
dies for you?

Now hands and mouth and straddle,

and what of the Big Bang—
dense heat and
burst,
dark matter
and microwaves?
When I get older,
I will get smaller,

but the universe
only expands.

And thrusts and claps,

and the God Particle
is not really God,
so where will I
find the father?
And why that metaphor
when no dad
worth the title
gets another chance
after a Katrina,
and a Middle Passage,
and boxcars,
and plague,
and Sand Creek
& Sandy Hook.

Oh, God,
Oh, God.

PART IV:
HOW TO READ A BEDTIME STORY

THE ER STAFF LISTENS TO MY HEART AND ME

I tell them it's a flutter
(because that's what I hear on TV),
but it's less Monarch, more bee
that swarms before death—then leaves.

Or maybe my chest is an elevator shaft
with a car packed full of children who
press each button to see the lights, hear the dings
until the cable snaps and they plummet.

My fear pushes the first beads of sweat out
and I've stepped from the shower onto
an electric bathmat, where I feel the surge
in each hair in my pits and around my nipples.

I explain that I get how the astronauts feel
when they drift, weightless, and look down at
home, knowing some bad math here, the pull
of the wrong lever there pushes them
        into eternal orbit.

But mostly, I say, I know what it's like to be lonely—
that when the end comes, we search our
hearts only to find each chamber empty.

WHEN YOU FIND ME WRITING IN THE COFFEE SHOP
(OR SLOWLY SINKING TO THE BOTTOM OF THE OCEAN)

I start to drown the second I nod a distracted hello
from behind my latté and laptop.
You set down *el té negro* and tell me
of your trip to Spain, kneeling to slip your
fisherman's knot around my ankles.
I already feel the saltwater slurry in my shoes,
but you tie on a rock for good measure.
At the pictures on your phone—
Sebastián, cathedral, tour guide, tapas—
the scuffed tile floor gives way to muck and current,
and the waves are over my head now.
My limbs flail toward the surface to salvage my
floating couplets, my waterlogged metaphors,
but I snag only kelp between my fingers.
Your muffled and muffling voice
documents my descent,
past starfish and sonnets,
devil rays and deadlines.
Pressure swells behind my sea-stung eyes
and stops up my ears—it's only Doppler now
as my limp body meets sandy floor.
Cause of death: poem interrupted.
But it's beautiful down here in the deep dark.
I will grow gills and call a silent shipwreck home.
I will listen to whales' laments and spend eternity
writing seductive seabed songs.

PLAYING 2ND TROMBONE ON DUKE ELLINGTON'S "BLUE FEELING"

doo be doo be do DWEE dah,
doo be dwee dah,
doo boo bop dwop dah;
doo boo deet dah bah
DWEE dah, DWEE dah, DWEE dah,
wah dah.

{rest}

HOW TO READ A SUNDIAL

a love story

At Sun's direction, Shadow makes his oblique journey.
He knows the route, nods to noon and two,
smiles as he turns past twins, six and nine.
He greets each day with unflagging joy,
relishes his role in the twelve-hour circuit.

Once, he had thought it would be better
if there were no Sun—that there'd be an
end to the tedious ecliptic which
mires him in monotony day after day.

But Sun's course is just prelude to Moon's moment,
a starry symphony that seems to suspend time,
and tells Shadow to lose himself in celestial beauty.

May we, too, smile through our solar sameness
for the promise of lasting lunar love.

ADAMAH

In the angle of twin morning rays,
I see your heart beating just under
the surface of your chest.

A font of energy bursts forth,
ripples over your skin,
like humans' subterranean beginnings.

> And you remind me that we are Earth people,
> formed with mud,
> that there's a world in me, too.

I would leave my own creation,
let it flame out, wither,
to rest in yours and find paradise.

> But you tell me I should nurture mine,
> press it close to you, and
> author new existence together.

Every genesis rouses chaos,
crafts beauty from mishmash,
sets spiraling spheres steady.

> Our bodies can too.

TO MY WIFE, MY LOVE, WHO BROUGHT HOME LITE MAYO

It's the little things, you say,
and you draw me to you,
touch our once-straight edges,
softened.
You press your ear to my heart,
which has had its episodes.
You lead me to the nursery, where
our son snores under soft crochet.
And you tell me you love me,
that we vowed old age.

But when I slice the cap off a ripe heirloom
and leave a tender trail of red with
each gushing stroke on worn butcher block,
I cannot help but think that we deserve
everything in its fullest.
Let this be my apology, then,
for the thick layers I will paint on
this bread and on the walls of our hearts.

OXYGEN MASK

Forgive the flight attendant when
she tells us in sleepy pantomime
that we must first secure our own
masks before assisting others. She
does not consider the hours we've
spent counting breaths from bassinets,
our midnight watchman-waiting for delicate
rise and fall, the mirrors under noses catching
vapors—puffs of assurance that disappear.
She forgets, perhaps, that air is but a
transfer from creator to created, and the
world is not yet through with our work.
Forgive her, for she does not know that
we have ripped out our own lungs and
ironed them flat every day of our new life
that we could endure a loss in cabin pressure.

PROGRESS

Columbus, Mississippi

They say there are cars
buried under Mag Bowl turf—
iron in gridiron soil.
Roaring twenties ruins
heaped and packed to fend off
Depression's trespass—
FDR's boys turning
loss into pigskin palace
for neighbors, rivals.

Now, concrete slab stands
split, make way for creeping weeds,
and forget Fridays.
Crowds have scattered to
their corners across town
where new bleachers
flaunt metallic shine.
Linemen's fingers dig,
twist into scrimmage line and
find nothing but dirt.

WHY I CAN'T LISTEN TO WEEZER'S BLUE ALBUM ANYMORE

Because I'm too old for vacant lots
and Malibu cut with Gatorade.
Because I can't stand the humidity
when the power windows are down.
Because they stopped making your
flavor of Lip Smackers, and we have
nothing left to explore, anyhow.
But also because when I saw you
yesterday, packing your trunk in
the Kroger parking lot, my stomach
knotted like it used to when you sang,
But you know I'm yours,
and I know you're mine,
and that's for all time.

LINES COMPOSED UPON HITTING REPLY ALL TO A FACULTY-WIDE EMAIL

I knew in a click I could never return.
I pulled sackcloth from my desk drawer
and without a word started my long, barefoot
march down scored mud-gravel roads and
into the wilderness.

There would be others, I thought:
the weatherman ignorant of a hot mic,
the lady who let a fart slip-squeak in church,
those whose emojis meant for partners
sent to parents.

Yes, it would be hard at first—
building the fires, whittling the fishing javelins—
but these would be my people: the bearded
and broken, the naked but unafraid
bedaubed in our unburdening.

Yes, we would renounce the before times,
choose new gods and place dried locusts on
now silent tongues. We'd spiral into the new
universes unraveling in each other's stares, and
there'd be no need for replies.

THOMAS RICHARDSON

THE HAIKUIST LIVE-TWEETS A ROAD TRIP DIAPER CHANGE

In rearview mirror,
baby's face scrunches, reddens.
No exit in sight.
#TheRoad
|

Grunts turn to giggles
as Daddy panic-fingers
stuck window button.
#shartenfreude
|

At rural Citgo,
changing tables withdrawn for
French tickler vending.
#nottickled #backtocar
|

Legs slip from Dad's hands.
Chubby feet catch used diaper,
Pollock-paint back seat.
#saveitforartschool
|

Wind tunnel kisses
bare bum, inspires golden stream.
Humble baptism.
#aspersion #affusion
|

Widened stance steadies
Dad for fresh attempt. A dive—
wrestle-wrapped success.
#smallvictory #needsink #ordrink
|

Baby strapped in Bjorn.
Stained father slinks back inside.
Soap lever pumps air.
#Sisyphus

On cockpit return,
Dad sheds clothes, weeps bosom
empty—turns toward home.
#sunset #neverforget

WRITING MY LAST WILL AND TESTAMENT BEFORE THE TOWN FESTIVAL FUN RUN
(OR WHEN I'M GLUE)

If I don't make it past the third turn,
if I tumble in a heap at the intersection
between the balloon animals and the
lemonade stand, give me the Eight Belles
treatment right there on the asphalt
then boil me down for glue. I've
worn down my joints in a hundred
healthy and unhealthy ways, but there
should be enough collagen left in
my tendons, my bones, my hide
to tack down that corner of formica
countertop I've promised to fix every Sunday
and napped instead. Maybe there will be
some remaining for a photo collage,
a snazzy spread of happy lies to
show the church ladies at the wake,
or to my son when he's old enough to
imagine me a hero. Or save some of me
for his science fair board—to adhere a
hypothesis or pie chart. For my mother's
sake, paint me on the weak spine of
my granddaddy's bible so that she can keep
tracing her finger along the jots and tittles
of his penciled marginalia. Whatever you do,
do not leave me on a shelf. Don't let me
dry up or crust over in a drawer until
I'm tossed out with the dead batteries.

A BEDTIME STORY

It was after the baby animal book
I promised I'd never die.
We read of joeys in pouches—
of their drinking, sleeping, waiting
for their wobbly legs to set and
spring them out on their own.
We learned of wolf cubs packed
warm in rocky dens, tasting
from adult mouths before
leading hunts on cold proving grounds.
We sang of water-swept otters
nurture-nestled in crooks of parents' arms
or holding hands with their own sleepy partners.
You, child and father of this man,
then asked behind searching blue eyes,
When I'm a daddy, will you be my little boy?
I could have left you with your visions, your
picture book sketches: bearing me
on your back through the wilderness,
laying me down in a nest you built by beak or paw.
I should have told you I can't wait to
shrink back to grub state, or to open my
mouth to your love-hunted offerings.
Instead, I chuckled my drowsy reply:
When you're a daddy, I'll be an old man.
Maybe I had my own picture book visions—
sweaters and bifocals, Buicks and booster seats
for after school pickups. I would read these
same books and feel this all over again.
But in just one beat you cut through my fog and
future fancy with another question—
And then you'll die?—and you burst into tears.
You can't die, you can't die, you can't,

you wailed while I sat silent and stupid and
fiddling through slick pages of cartoon critters.
I looked off and saw nothing but light and shadow.
Soothing songs sat thick in my throat.
I turned primate, pulled you in tighter,
kissed your head I held against my beating chest,
and fed you with the story you wanted to hear.

A PLEA TO THE REMNANTS

This is for you, my children, whom
I've so ingloriously abandoned:
the line I shipped to military school
because you weren't more like your brother,
the couplet I wired rent money so you'd stay away.

And this is for the kids still with me,
though no one really knows:
the metaphor hidden in the mother-in-law suite,
the conceit on the basement cot.

All my children, come—out of hiding,
without shame—just come home.
I will rend my clothing and beg forgiveness.
I will slay the fatted calf and play the harp for you.
We will feast and laugh, and in our joy
write the sonnets that make us whole.

SOMEDAY I'LL LOVE THOMAS RICHARDSON

after Ocean Vuong (after Roger Reeves after Frank O'Hara)

Thomas, step out of line.
The handkerchief, the parasol
will be there when it's time,
and the mourners will
go about the streets.
There is no devil in this town,
and you've made gods of niche
and urn and ash.
When the courthouse tower
strikes and chimes, lay down
the symbols, the fathers
and fathers in mechanical
succession to dust and silence.
Your father, your son,
your love still burns in
beatific vision on the
Dalí in your chest:
hot reds and golds
melting upward toward
piercing blue skies.
Take these love-fierce hands,
clamped like jaws of life, and crack
open the cavity, Thomas. Let burst
forth the fire that licks clean your
matted eyes and warms the feet of
freaks who dance and clap till morning.

CPSIA information can be obtained
at www.ICGtesting.com
Printed in the USA
FSHW011320230421